growth

A JOURNAL to WELCOME

PERSONAL CHANGE

SUSIE

GHAHREMANI

RB

ROOST BOOKS

Welcome

A JOURNAL CAN BE SO MUCH MORE than an OUTLET — it can also be a COMPANION, a RESOURCE, and a PLACE to FIND ANSWERS. I DISCOVERED the power of writing down intentions while navigating major changes in my life. RESEARCH confirms that PUTTING YOUR GOALS into WORDS helps you stay both mindful of your objectives and ACCOUNTABLE as you move toward them.

WRITING allows you to become more aware of your habits, your PRIORITIES, your THOUGHTS, and your OPPORTUNITIES. WITH YOUR PRACTICE and commitment, this journal will be a new SPACE for you to DAYDREAM, find SUPPORT and MOTIVATION, and RECORD your PERSONAL TRANSFORMATION. My HOPE is that someday you WILL LOOK BACK at this and see JUST HOW MUCH you've grown.

— susie

commitment

I'm making an effort to change and grow.

I will use this journal to inspire and track my progress.

_____

NAME / DATE

THE FUTURE IS THE RESULT OF WHAT WE DO RIGHT NOW.

— PEMA CHÖDRÖN

seed

SETTING GOALS

CLARITY and CERTAINTY are the
FOUNDATIONS of a commitment to
change. Use this section to SET
YOUR INTENTIONS and build your
unique path to success.

DEFINE YOUR GOALS
and gather sources of
MOTIVATION to support
you along the way.

DESCRIBE the CHANGE
you want to make in your life.

Where are you in this moment?

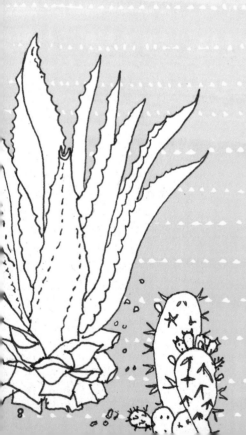

8

What are you thinking and feeling about the very idea of change?

WHY did you make this commitment to grow?

Reflect on the moment you began your journey and when the urge to take your first step arose.

_____

_____

_____

_____

_____

_____

_____

_____

_____

_____

_____

_____

_____

_____

_____

LIST

the reasons you want to make this shift in your life.

BECAUSE...

BECAUSE...

BECAUSE...

because...

BECAUSE...

Because...

Use open pages like
these to journal about
the present moment.
You can continue writing
about the prior questions
or simply share your
day or mindset.

WHEN YOU
UNDERSTAND
WHY YOU ARE
DOING SOMETHING,
IT IS EASY TO
EXERT YOURSELF
AT THE TASK.

— MOH HARDIN

What kind of SUPPORT will help you THRIVE?

WHAT ENVIRONMENT,

PEOPLE,

and THOUGHTS

make you feel CONFIDENT and CAPABLE?

WHAT HAS HELPED YOU SUCCEED in the PAST?

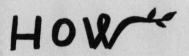

HOW CAN YOU REPEAT YOUR SUCCESS?

WHO

INSPIRES
YOU

and
WHY?

CULTIVATING SUPPORT

LIST the RESOURCES, BOOKS, CLASSES, STATISTICS, QUOTATIONS, and any INSPIRATION that will help you accomplish your goal here.

IMAGINE HOW YOU MIGHT feel as you accomplish the GOALS you've set for yourself.

- -

- -

- -

- -

- -

- -

DESCRIBE that FEELING IN A SINGLE WORD:

_____ .

USE this WORD as a MANTRA to INVOKE your intention and REMIND you of your larger goals.

TAKE SOME
TIME to
DRAW your
NEW MANTRA here

CUT THIS SECTION OUT
and CARRY it with you! PUT IT in YOUR WALLET OR on your COMPUTER to REMIND you of YOUR INTENTIONS.

JUST WHERE
YOU ARE —
THAT'S THE
PLACE TO START.

— PEMA CHÖDRÖN

WHO IN YOUR LIFE SUPPORTS YOU UNCONDITIONALLY?

WHO IN YOUR LIFE is COMMITTED to your SUCCESS?

CONSIDER SHARING YOUR GOALS with a FRIEND OR someone who WILL SUPPORT and CELEBRATE YOUR EFFORTS.

WHO HAS SUPPORTED your GROWTH in the PAST?

WHAT DID they DO to MAKE you FEEL ENCOURAGED?

PLEASE USE this SECTION AS A REMINDER TO SUPPORT YOURSELF as much as those who encourage you do.

LIFE IS HERE, IN EACH STEP.

— THICH NHAT HANH

SPROUT

GROWING YOUR EFFORTS

USE this space to create a
PLAN OF ACTION, LISTS, and
NOTES on your early progress.

REFER BACK to this Section to
track, inspire, and RECORD
your efforts.

THINK SMALL!

Not all change needs to come from big leaps. What daily choices might move you toward the change you want to make?

- _____

- _____

- _____

- _____

- _____

- _____

- _____

-

THINK FORWARD!

What can you accomplish in FIVE
MINUTES to move toward your goal?

_____

_____

_____

_____

TEN MINUTES? _____

_____

AN HOUR? _____

_____

_____

_____

THINK BIG!

How will you recognize your progress?
What milestones will signal that
you're moving toward your goal
in a few weeks or a few months?

- _____

- _____

- _____

- _____

- _____

- _____

- _____

- _____

THINK BACKWARD!

What steps will it take to get to your first milestone?
What small actions will you need to take to land there?

- [ ] _____
- [ ] _____
- [ ] _____
- [ ] _____
- [ ] _____
- [ ] _____
- [ ] _____

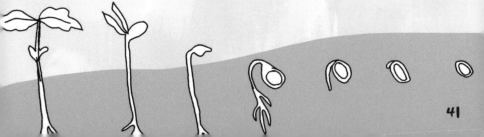

TODAY IS
    TODAY.
TODAY IS NOT
    TOMORROW.
TODAY IS
    ABSOLUTELY
        TODAY.

— SHUNRYŪ SUZUKI

What will you do **TODAY** to work on the transformation you're undertaking?

Make a commitment here.

44

REPEAT

YOUR INTENTIONS:

Throughout your day, bring to mind YOUR MANTRA (page 26) or remind yourself of your goal.

Pick some EVERYDAY ACTIVITIES or TIMES that you can use as a CUE to remember your commitment...

like WHEN YOU BRUSH YOUR TEETH,
before A MEAL, or BEFORE BED.

HAVE YOU FOUND THIS JOURNEY CHALLENGING
IN ANY WAY? WHY OR WHY NOT?

DO YOU REWARD YOURSELF FOR OVERCOMING
CHALLENGES and OBSTACLES? HOW?

THE WORLD
IS THE MOUNTAIN,
AND EACH ACTION,
THE SHOUT THAT
ECHOES BACK.

— RUMI

The WORK YOU'RE putting into achieving your own wishes may be empowering and REWARDING in ITSELF, but ACKNOWLEDGING and CELEBRATING your ACCOMPLISHMENTS is ALSO IMPORTANT!

HOW WILL you CELEBRATE the MILESTONES you defined on PAGE 40?

MILESTONE	REWARD	DATE ACCOMPLISHED

WHAT has SHIFTED —

in YOU, in YOUR LIFE, or AROUND YOU —

since you began this process?

BE AS SPECIFIC as possible.

WHAT will you do today
to work toward your goal?
CREATE YOUR PLAN
of ACTION here.

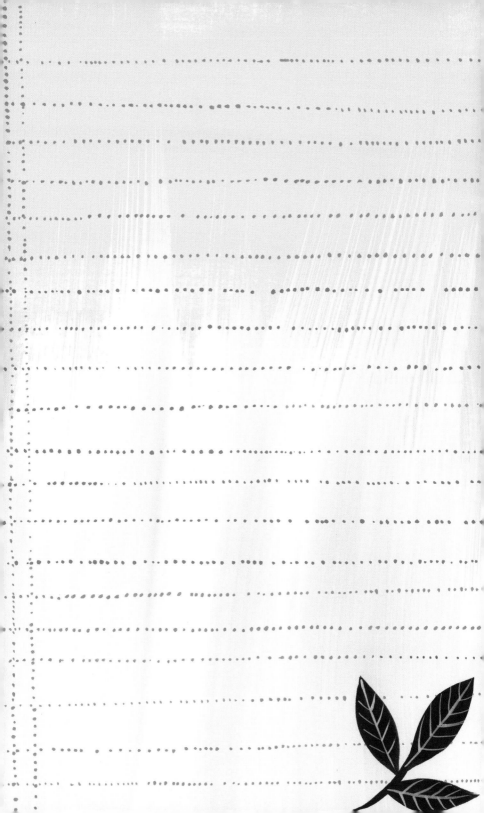

What do you HOPE
will happen as you
make this change
in your life

?

I hope...

I hope...

I hope...

SOME OF OUR ACTIONS AND EFFORTS ARE LIKE SEEDS. WE PLANT THEM NOW, AND THEY BEAR FRUIT AFTER MANY YEARS.

—GAVIN HARRISON

BLOOM

NURTURing MOMENTUM

MEANINGFUL CHANGE is a COMMITMENT
we RENEW to OURSELVES EVERY DAY.
USE this SPACE to DOCUMENT and REFLECT
on your STRIDES, persistence, and hopes.

Use this section
to STRENGTHEN
your resolve,
patience, and
commitment.

LOOK
BACK AT THE MANTRA YOU
CAME UP WITH ON PAGE 26.
WHAT DOES THIS WORD MEAN to you NOW?

REWRITE YOUR MANTRA HERE.

_____

SPEND TIME FORMING EACH LETTER WITH CARE.

IF YOU'RE IN NEED OF A NEW MANTRA, TAKE the TIME to COME UP WITH ONE NOW.

I'M CREATING
MY FUTURE WITH
EVERY WORD,
EVERY ACTION,
EVERY THOUGHT.

— PEMA CHÖDRÖN

GROWTH CHART

DRAW YOUR PROGRESS.

WHERE
YOU
BEGAN

WHERE
YOU'LL
GO

WHERE ARE YOU NOW?
DRAW HERE.

WHAT are TEN POSITIVE THINGS that have occurred since you began working toward this CHANGE?

1

2

3

4

5

6

7

8

10

9

WHAT is something NEW you've tried as a result of your efforts to grow?

HAVE your resolutions
shifted from your
declaration at the
start of this process?
WHAT has changed
and WHY?

REFLECT here.

What
SMALL
HABITS

can you
incorporate
into your
daily life
to keep
your goal
moving
forward ?

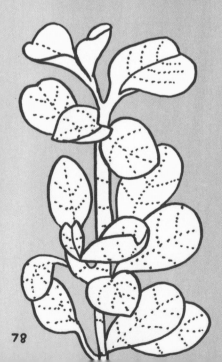

MAKE A LIST

of WORDS that describe
YOUR EFFORTS to change:

_____

_____

_____

_____

_____

_____

_____

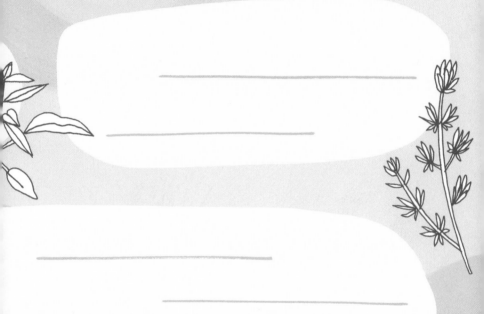

_____

_____

_____

_____

_____

NOW CIRCLE

the WORDS that MOTIVATE you to KEEP GOING, the words that tell you you're on the right path. LISTEN to THOSE.

IN THE WEEDS...

FILL out this TO-DO LIST of SMALL STEPS YOU CAN TAKE **THIS** **WEEK** to move toward your goal.

- ○
- ○
- ○
- ○
- ○
- ○
- ○
- ○
- ○
- ○
- ○

PLANT NEW SEEDS

FILL OUT THIS TO-DO LIST of
BIG STEPS you can make
in the FUTURE to move
toward your goal.

_____ ◯
_____ ◯
_____ ◯
_____ ◯
_____ ◯
_____ ◯
_____ ◯
_____ ◯
_____ ◯

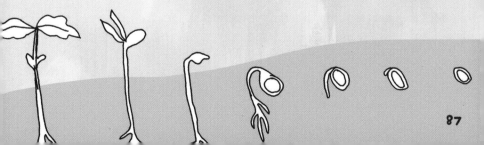

WHAT will
your next MILESTONE BE?

DESCRIBE
YOUR PATH to GET THERE.

DESCRIBE TODAY in ONE WORD:

WHY DID you CHOOSE that WORD?

WHO HAS BEEN an ADVOCATE, FRIEND,

MENTOR, or INSPIRATION

to YOU as YOU'VE WORKED On YOUR GOAL?

HOW HAS THIS PERSON

SUPPORTED YOUR DEVELOPMENT?

IN THE WEEDS...

FILL out this TO-DO LIST of
SMALL STEPS YOU CAN TAKE **THIS**
WEEK to move toward your goal.

- ◯
- ◯
- ◯
- ◯
- ◯
- ◯
- ◯
- ◯
- ◯
- ◯
- ◯

PLANT NEW SEEDS

FILL OUT THIS TO-DO LIST of
BIG STEPS you can make
in the FUTURE to move
toward your goal.

- [ ]
- [ ]
- [ ]
- [ ]
- [ ]
- [ ]
- [ ]
- [ ]
- [ ]

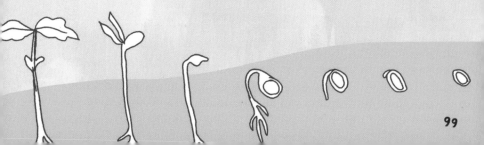

GROWTH CHART

DRAW YOUR PROGRESS.

WHERE
YOU
BEGAN

WHERE ARE YOU NOW?
DRAW HERE.

WHERE
YOU'LL
GO

TODAY

I AM
GRATEFUL
FOR...

IN THE WEEDS...

FILL out this TO-DO LIST of SMALL STEPS YOU CAN TAKE THIS WEEK to move toward your goal.

○ _____

○ _____

○ _____

○ _____

○ _____

○ _____

○ _____

○ _____

○ _____

○ _____

○ _____

PLANT NEW SEEDS

FILL OUT THIS TO-DO LIST of BIG STEPS you can make in the FUTURE to move toward your goal.

- [ ]
- [ ]
- [ ]
- [ ]
- [ ]
- [ ]
- [ ]
- [ ]
- [ ]

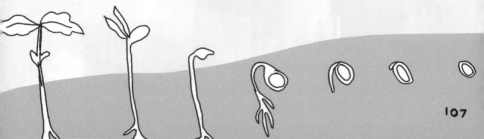

OUR JOURNEY CONSISTS OF CONSTANT UPS AND DOWNS, HOPE AND FEAR, BUT IT IS A GOOD JOURNEY.

—CHÖGYAM TRUNGPA

ThRive

REFLECTING ON GROWTH

USE this SECTION to REFLECT on your achievements and STRIDES!

REFER BACK to this section to appreciate and acknowledge your CONTINUED PROGRESS.

HAS WORKING ON YOUR GOAL BECOME
A HABIT? HOW DO YOU REMIND YOURSELF
DAILY of YOUR COMMITMENT?

ARE YOU CONSCIOUS OF YOUR GOAL every day?
IF NOT, what might help you renew
this COMMITMENT TO YOURSELF daily?

ARE you
MAKING PROGRESS
as you PLANNED
and EXPECTED?

IF SO, HOW DOES it FEEL to REALIZE your objectives?

IF NOT, can you FORGIVE YOURSELF and get BACK ON TRACK or make a new plan?

What might that look like?

WHAT WILL YOU DO TODAY to WORK TOWARD YOUR GOAL? Make a commitment here.

WHEN WILL YOU KNOW
YOU'VE MET YOUR GOAL?

WHAT WILL YOUR FINAL
MILESTONE BE?

WHAT'S YOUR PLAN
to GET THERE?

TAKE ROOT...

LIST all the ways you've
changed during
this process.

-
-
-
-
-
-
-
-
-
-
-
-
-
-
-

AND GROW

LIST any
MILESTONES
you'd still like
to reach.

○ _____

○ _____

○ _____

○ _____

○ _____

_____

○ _____

○ _____

NOTES ON CHANGE

FLIP back through this journal and read some of what you've written.

REFLECT on the progress you've made so far.

How DOES it FEEL to stand where you are now relative to where you started?

A FLOWER
NEEDS SUNSHINE
TOGETHER WITH
RAINDROPS
TO BLOSSOM
SO BEAUTIFULLY.

— CHÖGYAM TRUNGPA

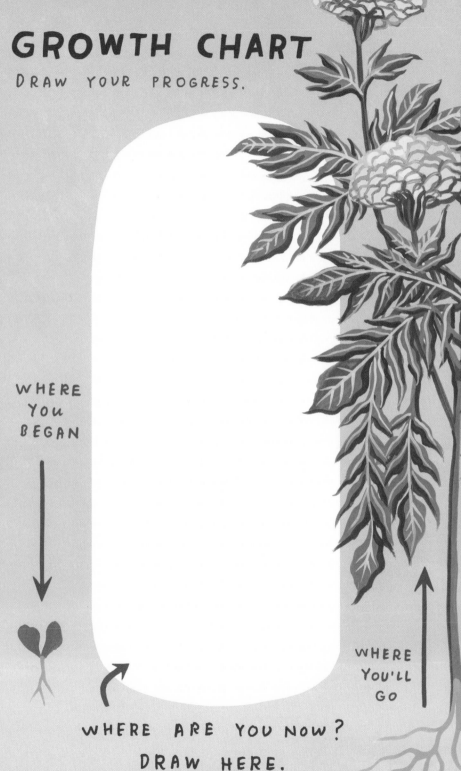

GROWTH CHART
DRAW YOUR PROGRESS.

WHERE
YOU
BEGAN

WHERE ARE YOU NOW?
DRAW HERE.

WHERE
YOU'LL
GO

BRANCHING OUT:

WHAT'S NEXT FOR YOU?

HOW WILL YOU KEEP UP the MOMENTUM YOU'VE BUILT SO YOU can CONTINUE to THRIVE?

133

WE CAN'T SEE WHERE
WE'RE HEADED, ONLY
WHERE WE'VE BEEN.

— PEMA CHÖDRÖN

REFLECTING on GROWTH:

WHAT have you learned about YOURSELF during this JOURNEY? RE-READ YOUR NOTES from the PROMPTS on pages 8-9. HOW HAVE your feelings about the VERY IDEA of CHANGE evolved?

CREDITS AND RESOURCES

THE QUOTATIONS in this book are included with kind permission from the following sources:

ROOST BOOKS
An Imprint of Shambhala Publications, Inc.
2129 13th Street
Boulder, Colorado 80302
roostbooks.com

9 8 7 6 5 4 3 2

Printed in SINGAPORE

SHAMBHALA PUBLICATIONS makes every effort to print on acid-free, recycled paper.

Roost Books is distributed worldwide by Penguin Random House, Inc., and its subsidiaries.

LIBRARY of Congress CATALOGING-in-Publication Data
NAMES: GHAHREMANI, SUSIE, AUTHOR.
TITLE: GROWTH: A JOURNAL to WELCOME PERSONAL CHANGE / SUSIE GHAHREMANI.
DESCRIPTION: First edition. | Boulder, Colorado: ROOST BOOKS, an imprint of Shambhala Publications, Inc., [2020] | Includes bibliographical references.
IDENTIFIERS: LCCN 2019052789 | ISBN 9781611808025 (trade paperback)
SUBJECTS: LCSH: DIARIES — AUTHORSHIP — Psychological Aspects. | DIARIES — Authorship. DIARIES — THERAPEUTIC USE. | SELF-ACTUALIZATION (PSYCHOLOGY) | CHANGE.
CLASSIFICATION: LCC PN4390 .G47 2020 | DDC 158.1/6 — dc23
LC RECORD AVAILABLE at https://lccn.loc.gov/2019052789